YOUR POCKET GUIDE TO

GREAT GAMES FOR GOLF

YOUR POCKET GUIDE TO

GREAT GAMES FOR GOLF

By Tom Newton

GRAVITY RESOURCES, LLC
P.O. BOX 785
LAKE OSWEGO, OR 97034
www.greatgamesforgolf.com

ISBN: 0-9725169-0-5

Printed in the United States of America.
Designed by Bailey/Franklin, Portland, Oregon.

Gravity Resources, LLC
P.O. Box 785
Lake Oswego, OR 97034
www.greatgamesforgolf.com

Dedicated to my wife

CHERI

Whose loving support of all
my crazy ideas
enriches my life!

CONTENTS

INTRODUCTION

Your Pocket Guide to Great Games for Golf is designed for anyone who loves golf and appreciates additional challenges in a round. A little side game has the benefit of improving your focus on the game and providing great entertainment (not to mention picking up a couple bucks from your buddies).

Most of the games in this book are designed to allow you to maintain a legitimate score for posting. Game scores can be kept separately so you can post a score for your handicap.

A WORD ON HANDICAPS

The games in this guide may be played with either your actual score on each hole (gross) or by adjusting your score with a handicap (net).

The majority of the games are described using a net scoring basis. The gods of golf (a.k.a. United States Golf Association) have gone to a lot of trouble to create a game where you can compete with anyone else on an equal basis, so let's use it. They say; *"The USGA Course Rating System ensures that golf courses are rated in relation to all other courses. The System adjusts a player's USGA Handicap Index according to the difficulty of a course. As a result, no matter who golfers play with—or where they play—they can enjoy a fair game."* By the way, can you think of any other sport where you can do this?!

···

If your playing partners don't have handicaps, simply play with your gross scores, or estimate your average score and negotiate some reasonable arrangement. In this event, it is good to agree to reassess after the first nine holes.

If you would like to create an official handicap for you and your playing partners, you can establish your own golf club with the help of the USGA. Here's what they say:

"Forming a golf club is not at all difficult. The USGA Handicap system defines a golf club as an organization of individual members with committees appointed to supervise golf activities and to maintain the integrity of the USGA Handicap System. The club membership requirement is an essential part of the USGA Handicap System. A club's members must have a reasonable and regular opportunity to play golf with each other, and must be able personally to return scores or scorecards for posting. The club membership requirement is an essential part of the USGA Handicap System to provide "peer review" to protect the integrity and reliability of USGA Handicap Indexes.

An organization of amateur golfers at a public course is considered a golf club if it satisfies the above conditions. If a "golf club" which issues USGA Handicaps is not readily available to you, you can create such a club or a golf club without Real Estate can be created. You can form a club

....

with a minimum of ten golfers. The club can be formed from business associates or just golfing friends, provided that they live in a close geographic area and play golf regularly together."

Learn how to form your own golf club by visiting http://www.usga.org/handicap/establish/index.html.

Or email the USGA at handicap@usga.org with your name and address to receive a FREE Club Formation Kit. Put "Club Formation Kit" in the subject heading of the email.

Finally, this guide is not intended to be a "rule book" for games, but rather a resource to give you ideas, and resources to create your own versions of *great games for golf*. There are numerous variations and interpretations in side games. You may have knowledge of some of the games described within and find they are not described exactly as you know them. I have described each in the way I like to play them, and left them general enough for you to add any modifications you like. In fact, if you have a great idea to improve any game, or a new game you would like to share with the world, please visit our website (**www.greatgamesforgolf.com**) and click to the page "Game Feedback." Your contribution* may be included in our next edition of *Great Games for Golf*, and may even win a prize!

*Note: All game ideas submitted become the exclusive property of Gravity Resources, LLC.

PART 1
Traditional Formats

A BRIEF EXPLANATION OF SOME OF THE
BEST KNOWN COMPETITIVE FORMATS

STROKE (MEDAL) PLAY

TOTAL SCORE FOR THE ROUND VERSUS YOUR OPPONENT(S)

Compete against your opponent for the lowest total score for the round (the same way the pros play). Handicaps can be used to create parity between the players. Each player's handicap is subtracted from the gross score to result in a net score that is compared with the net score of the other player(s) at the completion of the round.

There are several ways you can play partners using Stroke Play. For example, partners can use their best **low net best ball*** on each hole to make a team score to compete against another team.

Or, play a **high/low** two person team game. To score this format, the net lower individual scores compete against the net individual higher scores on each hole. Handicaps are used by adding each team's handicaps together and subtracting the difference. The team which has more handicap strokes use them for the **high ball*** score on the hardest holes as indicated on the score card.

Players can bet a set amount of money for the low net 18-hole score. Or, as a team, bet on the difference between each team's score with a dollar value on each stroke.

*Note: The term **best ball** is often misunderstood. In this book, best ball is the lowest score posted on any given hole by an individual or team. Conversely, **high ball** will always refer to the highest score for the team per hole.

MATCH PLAY

PLAYING TO WIN INDIVIDUAL HOLES

This game is played by matching strokes with your opponent, hole by hole. The goal is to win the most holes. The winner of each hole is the player with the lowest net score on that hole. When a player wins a hole, they go **one-up**. A hole that is tied is **halved**. The player who has the most holes won at the end of the round is the victor. When a player has won enough holes that their opponent, even by winning every remaining hole can only tie, the match is **dormey**. Once a player has won enough holes that they cannot be beat, the match is over (although most people play out).

In Match Play a player's total gross score does not dictate winning or losing. What does matter is how you score on each hole compared to your opponent. So you can have a couple of bad holes and still win. This is why the game is so well liked by amateurs.

The game is best played with handicaps. The player with the lower handicap gives the player with the higher handicap strokes equaling the difference between their handicaps. For example, if the better player is a 10 handicap and their opponent is a 15, the high-handicap player would receive a stroke on the five most difficult holes as indicated on the scorecard.

SCRAMBLE

**PLAYERS USE EACH OTHER'S BEST SHOTS TO
EARN THE LOWEST POSSIBLE TEAM SCORE**

Each player on the team (usually a foursome) hits his
tee shot. The group selects the best shot and the
remaining players pick up and hit from that location.
Players continue hitting each shot and selecting the best
result all the way into the hole.

The area of play from each fairway location is within
one club length—no closer to the hole from the
selected best shot. You are not allowed to improve the
condition of the lie by using the one club length rule to
escape from the rough or a sand trap. On the green,
you are allowed to place your ball and putt within six
inches from the location of the best shot, no closer to
the hole.

The team's best shots are used to create one combined group 18-hole score that competes with all other
participating teams.

SHAMBLE

PLAYERS PICK THE BEST DRIVE AND PLAY FROM THERE FOR A "BEST BALL" SCORE.

This game is similar to a *Scramble* (page 4) except that the best drive on each hole is the only shot for all to play. The team selects the best drive of the group and everyone hits their second shot from that location. From then on, each person must play their own ball all the way to the hole. Competition is usually scored using the best ball (lowest individual score) of the group on each hole.

SKINS / INDIVIDUAL PLAY

MONEY TO BE WON ON EVERY HOLE FOR THE LOWEST SCORE

The player who posts the single lowest score on each hole (without being tied or beaten by another player) wins one **skin**. In this game, if two tie, then all tie.

Use of handicaps is optional, but recommended whenever there is a discrepancy of more than four strokes between opponents. Many people believe that a higher handicap player has an advantage and recommend use of only one-half a person's handicap. You will have to negotiate what you think is fair in your group.

In this game, you can also play carryovers. If no one earns a skin on a particular hole, then on the next hole the player who gets a skin also gets a carryover skin from the previous hole(s). Another option is to double the dollar value of the skin on the second nine.

SKINS / MULTIPLE GROUPS

MONEY WON ON EVERY HOLE FOR LOW SCORE AMONG ALL

Several foursomes can enjoy a group skins game. Everyone who is in the skins game contributes an agreed amount into the pot. After the round is complete, the organizer runs down the scores on each hole to identify winners on various holes. The total number of skins won for the entire group is divided by the dollars in the pot to determine the value of each skin. In larger groups it works best to pay one skin for holes won with a par, two skins for holes won with a birdie and three skins won with an eagle or better. Carryovers stay at one skin each in this format.

If you wish to organize a large number of players who have varying handicaps, the game is most fair if you divide the group in two: one low handicap group and one high handicap group. The low group can play gross with the high group playing net.

NASSAU

DIVIDING THE MATCH INTO THREE COMPETITIVE SEGMENTS

Undisputedly the most popular weekend betting golf game, a Nassau is basically three matches inside of a round. Competitors attempt to win any of three segments of the game: 1) the front nine holes, 2) the back nine holes, and 3) the 18-hole total. So, if a player is playing a $2 Nassau, the front side is played for $2, the back side is played for $2 and the total worth $2. $6 total to be won or lost.

The most typical Nassau bet is based on Stroke Play with **net scores**. Match Play is an option; each player attempts to win individual holes and have more total won holes than their opponent in any or all of the three segments. No points are awarded for halved holes. In either format, if competitors come out even, then that segment is a push, and no one wins.

When playing a Nassau with partners, it is most common to play to use the **best net score** of the partners versus that of your opponents. Or, you can create a "points" version where you can win 2 points on each hole; 1 point for the lowest score and 1 point for the low total combined team score. The advantage of playing for points is that it keeps everyone in the match. Another version would be **high/low** where you simply match the two lowest scores against the two highest scores with each being worth a point.

CHAPMAN

TEAMMATES PLAY EACH OTHER'S SHOTS FOR TWO STROKES AND THEN ALTERNATE ON ONE BALL

Played with two person teams, each player hits his drive then plays his second shot by hitting his partner's ball. The best second shot of the two becomes then the only ball in play. From that location, the player whose shot is not used hits the first alternating shot.

Teammates continue hitting alternating shots on that one ball until holed.

This format can be played on all eighteen holes, or you can modify the number of dual shots hit on Par 3s and Par 5s. In this format, alternating shots begin after the drive on Par 3s and after three shots each on Par 5s.

CALLOWAY

A TOURNAMENT WHERE A FORMULA SETS YOUR HANDICAP/SCORE FOR THAT DAY.

This scoring system is used primarily for tournaments where there are a number of relatively inexperienced players involved. In such a tournament, many players may not have an established handicap so the format attempts to create a fair handicapping system.

We won't explain all the details here, but for your enlightenment, you only need to understand that a number of your worst holes are deducted or adjusted from the first 16 holes played.

For example, if you have a score in the 70s, you may deduct or adjust off one of your worst holes. If you score over 100, you may end up deducting or adjusting off your worst 4 holes. There are tables and calculations used to determine exactly how this works. You can find more information on the Internet on how to use this scoring system. Simply do a search using the words "calloway+golf+scoring".

STABLEFORD

A SCORING SYSTEM WHERE COMPETITORS WIN OR LOSE POINTS BASED ON HOLE SCORE

This is an individual tournament format where each player attempts to accumulate the most points. Points are won or lost as follows:

Double Eagle	8 points
Eagle	5 points
Birdie	2 points
Par	0 points
Bogey	-1 point
Double Bogey (or worse)	-2 points

The tournament is typically played with gross scores, but can easily be done on a net basis. Dollar amounts can be established for each point prior to the match to put a little skin in the game.

THE PRESS

A **press** is a new bet made during a match in addition to the original bet by the player or team that is losing. The **press bet** is most common in a Nassau (page 8) match, but can be used in any betting game with a little creativity.

A press means the original bet is doubled for the number of holes remaining from where the press was declared. This usually occurs when a player who is losing starts another bet hoping to offset the one he has already lost. Rules for calling a press should be agreed upon before the match begins.

It is common practice to declare an **automatic press** bet when a player or team is two down. The player or team that is ahead has the option of declining to accept the press, but it is customary to accept it. It is best practice to start a new line on the scorecard to record the press bet.

A different way to handle a press is to concede the original bet when it appears the contest is decided, and then the press represents a new bet for the same $ or more, played over the remaining holes.

POINT EARNING OPPORTUNITIES

USE THESE EVENTS TO AWARD POINTS DURING ANY GAME

At the beginning of your match for the day, these events can be used to add more challenge to your round. Points ($$) can be awarded to any player achieving the following:

Hole In One
Eagle
Birdie
Chip In
Long Drive
Sandy (par from sand trap)
One Putt (par or better)
Woody (par—hitting a tree)
Double Sandy (par from 2 bunkers)
KP on Par 4s and 5s (must be on in regulation)
Closest to the Pin on Par 3s (must make Par to win)
Polie (putts longer than the flagpole)
Coast Guard (par after landing in the water)
Arnie (par from the rough)

You can creatively add these point-earning opportunities to any game to add variety.

PART 2
Small Group Games

EASY GAMES TO ORGANIZE ON SHORT NOTICE

Look for these symbols that identify the options for number of participants:

          ♟ = Individuals

        ♟♟ = Partners in foursomes

    ♟♟♟♟ = Groups in foursomes

BINGO BANGO BONGO   👤

WIN WITH SKILLS IN VARIOUS ASPECTS OF THE GAME

This challenge puts separate values on the **long game**, **short game**, and **putting**. Three points are up for grabs on each hole. Points are given a dollar amount before the match begins.

The player who makes the putting surface first with the fewest strokes wins the 1st point.

After everyone is on the green, players putt in order. The longest putt wins a 2nd point.

The 3rd point is awarded to the player with the lowest net score on the hole. Points are tallied at the end of the game and the difference is paid out accordingly.

Many variations can be created here. Some like to play that a point is made for getting the ball closest to the hole in regulation.*

*Regulation means being on the green after one stroke on a Par 3, two on Par 4s, and three on Par 5s.

BLIND HOLES 🚶 🚶🚶 🚶🚶🚶🚶

RANDOM HOLES ARE OMITTED TO ESTABLISH YOUR FINAL SCORE

The goal in this game is to post the best total score possible after scores on three holes are randomly omitted. This adds an element of chance to the game. After the competition is set up as either individual or teams and the dollar buy-in agreed upon, play begins without anyone knowing which holes will be omitted. The game is played net with each person or team posting their best score on each hole.

At the conclusion of the round, a blind draw establishes which holes will be omitted from the scores. Once the total score is adjusted to the remaining 15 holes, the winners are declared. Pay out is usually win/place/show for groups of 12 or more.

BOGER 👤

POINTS ARE LOST TO YOUR OPPONENTS WHEN YOU MAKE NET BOGEY OR WORSE

The object in this game is to avoid giving points away. The first player to make a net bogey or worse owes each of their opponents a point. That person continues losing a point on every hole until 1) someone else bogeys, or 2) they themselves make a birdie.

If more than one person bogeys a hole, each of them pays the remaining players and the last bogey is on the hook for the next hole. Be careful to follow the rules for order of play as someone might get cranky. (Good to agree on this before the round begins.)

DEFENDER

EARN POINTS BY PROTECTING YOUR DESIGNATED HOLES

Each player is required to defend a group of holes to earn points. Use of net scores is most common. One player is designated as the Defender for each hole before the round begins. This can be done on a rotating basis, blind draw, or by assigning holes based on handicaps. (The lower handicaps protect the hardest holes.) 2 points are awarded if the defender wins the hole, 1 point for a tie, and 1 point given to all opponents if the defender loses the hole.

DICTATOR ⫯

BEAT YOUR PARTNERS ON A HOLE AND BECOME THE DICTATOR IN ORDER TO EARN POINTS

The goal is to win a hole outright and become the Dictator. Only the Dictator can win points. The game is best played in Match Play format (page 3) with handicaps. Handicap strokes are best taken against the lowest handicapper, who plays against par. Each player's handicap score adjustments are taken on the stroke index holes as indicated on the scorecard. For example, if you are to receive five strokes from your opponent, you take them on the five hardest holes shown on the card.

The first player to win a hole becomes the Dictator. To win points, the Dictator must win the next hole while holding the title. He continues holding the Dictator position by winning or halving holes. As soon as another player wins a hole outright, he owns the Dictator title. This is a great game to add other point winning opportunities. (See page 13.)

EASTWOOD 👤

THE GOOD, THE BAD AND THE UGLY

This is a point game where good is rewarded and bad is penalized. Players attempt to accumulate the most points with gains and losses scored as follows:

POINTS EARNED

Birdie or better	3 points
Par	2 points
Sandy	1 point
KP	1 point

POINTS LOST

Drive in rough	-1 point
Three Putt	-1 point
Bogey	-2 points
Double Bogey (or worse)	-3 points

Eastwood is a great game that helps everyone focus on good shot making.

FIVERS

FIVE POSSIBLE POINTS UP FOR GRABS ON EACH HOLE

A simple point game played with any number of opponents. There are five possible points available on any given hole:

Low net score	1 point
KP when on in regulation	1 point
Birdie	1 point
Polie	1 point
Sandy	1 point

Fivers can also be played in a partner/team format.

HOT POTATO 🧍 🧍🧍

WIN OR LOSE BY NOT POSTING THE WORST SCORE

Rotating players hold the **hot potato** on each tee, and must score better than the worst of the remaining players in the foursome to avoid losing points.

Choose a fixed order for teeing off before starting the round and follow it throughout the 18-hole match. The first person to tee off on each hole is designated to hold the hot potato on each hole. If his net score is not the worst, he wins a point. If it is the worst score, a point each is earned by each of his competitors. No points are earned or lost for halving a hole. In this game if the person with the hot potato ties anyone, there are no points lost.

THE HUNTED 🕴

A THREESOME GAME WHERE EACH HOLE PITS ONE AGAINST TWO

Each hole will pit one player against two **hunters**. The golfer with the middle-distance drive on each hole is on the run and the other two are in pursuit. (The middle KP ball on Par 3s.) The **hunted** player matches twice his net score on the hole against the combined net score of the hunters.

A dollar value is assigned to be at stake for each hole. For example, if each hole is worth a dollar and the hunters win, the loser owes them each $1. If the player on the run wins, he will collect $2. Decide in advance if the value of halved holes are carried over. Play honors on the tee. If you have one player who is consistently long, use the middle drive on hole number 1 and 10 to decide who is on the run, and then tee off in rotation for each hole from there.

NINES ♟

THREESOMES COMPETE BY EARNING POINTS ON EACH HOLE BASED ON RELATIVE SCORES

There are 9 points available on each hole and the group decides the dollar value for each point prior starting their round. Points are distributed after the conclusion of each hole according to each player's relative score as follows:

Lowest score	5 points
2nd lowest score	3 points
Highest score	1 point
Two tie for low score	4 points each
Two tie for 2nd lowest score	2 points each
All tie	3 points each

This game is easy to adapt for a foursome by simply changing the total points available and calling it *Twelves*. For this format:

Lowest score	6 points
2nd lowest score	4 points
3rd lowest score	2 points
Highest score	0 points

It's easy to figure out the math from there for all the possible outcomes in a foursome.

NINETY-NINE ♀ ♀♀

(NOT TO BE CONFUSED WITH NINES)
2-PERSON TEAMS—EACH PLAYER IS RESPONSIBLE
FOR SCORES ON 9 HOLES ONLY

This is a strategy best ball game in partner format in multiple teams. Each player is responsible to post a net score on 9 holes of the 18-hole match. Teammates choose which player posts a score on each hole as the round progresses. After holing out and before teeing off on the next hole, the team decides which partner's score to post on the card. This continues until either player has posted a total of 9 holes. Scores on the remaining holes must then be completed by the partner.

Winning the game requires good judgment and strategy. For example, it might be smarter to post a par from the higher handicapper than a birdie from the lower because the lower handicapper is more likely to score pars through the round.

PAR OR BETTER 👤 👥 👤👤👤👤

ONLY SCORE YOUR GOOD HOLES

Just to mix it up a bit, try competition where your final score is the number of holes in which you scored a net par or better. The high total wins.

For example, if you had six holes where you scored net bogey or worse, your final score would be 12 (18 – 6). If your opponent had eight bogeys, their score would be 10 (18-8) and you win!

This game is great for mid-handicappers as it focuses on potential, omitting bad holes completely.

PLAYERS CHOICE � ♟ ♟♟ ♟♟♟♟

PLAYERS USE THEIR HANDICAP STROKES WHEN AND WHERE THEY CHOOSE IN MATCH PLAY

In this game, all competitors use their handicaps in Match Play format (page 3) with one critical difference—they get to choose when they use their handicap allocation as the game progresses. So a twelve handicapper has twelve strokes to use in any combination on any given hole on the course. After each hole—and before teeing off on the next hole—each player declares how many of their handicap strokes they wish to use on the last completed hole.

For example, if a player has 5 strokes on a Par 3, they may choose to use 2 handicap strokes to make par. The game is best played with each player using his total number of handicap strokes, but can be even more strategic if you just use the stroke difference between opponents.

Be careful to keep accurate notes on your scorecard, and don't use up your strokes too early!

PROGRESSIVE NET 👤👤👤👤

TEAMS ATTEMPT TO POST THE BEST SCORES WITH PROGRESSIVELY MORE BALLS IN PLAY

Teams compete to accumulate the best score on a hole by adding their individual scores together. The game can be scored using either net or gross results. At first only one teammate's score counts, but as the game progresses, more players must contribute as follows: **one** ball is recorded for the first six holes, **two** balls are scored for the next six holes, and finally the **three** best balls are scored for the remaining six holes. The team with the best aggregate total wins the pot.

PUTT MASTERS   ♟   ♟♟   ♟♟♟♟

ADD YOUR NUMBER OF PUTTS TO YOUR HOLE SCORE

This scoring game is based on players adding their best net score to the number of putts on each hole. The lowest score wins.

For example, if you score par with a one putt on a Par 5 where you have a stroke; your score would be 5 (4 for a net birdie plus 1 for a single putt). If your opponent also had a stroke on the hole and also scored par but did so with 2 putts, his/her score would be a 6 (4 for a net birdie plus 2 two putts). This is a good game to play in Nassau format so you can have a winner for the front, back, and total score. For group play, simply score the best ball.

PLAYERS EARN POINTS FOR GOOD SHOT MAKING

This is a great game for less experienced golfers because it encourages smart play. Players are awarded one point every time they hit fairways on their drive for Par 4s and 5s. Points are also awarded for hitting the green in regulation. Another point is earned for making par or better.

Several variations can keep it interesting. For example, if more than one player qualifies on a hole, call it a carryover. Or, a carryover can be called if no one makes it, so that the point is available on the next fairway or green. For even more challenge, stipulate that **fairway** points require players stay in the fairway and make the green in regulation to qualify. Likewise, require players to make at least par to earn the point for hitting the green on Par 3s.

ROTATION ♗

GET A NEW PARTNER EVERY THREE HOLES AND ATTEMPT TO EARN POINTS

This game is won by collecting the greatest number points while rotating partners on every hole. Handicaps are used and strokes are taken on the stroke index holes.

The play goes like this: Player 1 tees off on the first hole with Player 2 and they play against Players 3 and 4. The pair who attains the best net combined score on the hole wins a point each. On the next hole, 1 plays with 3 against 2 and 4, and so on. No points are awarded for halved holes.

The game can also be played by rotating partners every six holes, but it's a bit less exciting.

THE SHEL GAME 🕴

PLAYERS TRY TO WIN THE PAR 3s, PAR 4s, AND PAR 5s SEPARATELY SCORED

This competition is divided into three hole segments and paid out three ways. Players agree on the dollar buy-in and pick teams or order of play before the round begins. Once play begins, scores on Par 4s, Par 3s, and Par 5s are kept separately. The best total net score (individual or team) for each segment wins a pot paid out as follows: 50% of the pot to the team with the best total score on Par 4s, 30% for the best score on Par 5s, and 20% on Par 3s. Some like to stipulate that in team play, a team can only win one of the three segments. If two segments are won, the lowest value segment goes to the second place team.

TRIPLE DOWN 🧍 🧍🧍

HOLD THE TEE AND WIN A POINT / LOSE AND IT COSTS THREE

Played individually, or as partners, the game starts by using a random method of deciding who gets the honor on the first tee. For an individual game, the person who tees off first tries to hold the tee for the next hole by making the best score on the first hole. Scoring can be either net or gross. If he does, he wins **one point**. If he loses the hole, **three points** are awarded to his opponents (one each). If the hole is halved, no points are awarded and the same player keeps the honor on the next hole.

In a team format, you still award one point for winning and give three points for losing, the players just share the outcome.

A dollar amount is assigned at the beginning of the round and points are totaled to decide who wins. This can also be played where partners rotate on each hole.

VARSITY 🚶 🚶🚶 🚶🚶🚶🚶

PICK A BALL TO SCORE AFTER INITIAL SHOTS ARE MADE ON EACH HOLE

This format can be used as a variation for any number of multiple team games. Partners choose which player's ball will count on each hole in the following pattern: after the team tees off on Par 3s, after the team has hit their second shot on Par 4s, and after the third shot after Par 5s. The player who's ball is used is on **varsity** the others are **jv**.

For example, two-person teams in a foursome would tee off on a Par 4. After everyone hits their second shot, one person on each team is declared to be the ball in play (on varsity). The other two become the Junior varsity team for the competition on that hole. The two Varsity players compete to make the best net score and win the hole for the team.

In four-person teams with multiple groups, the game is most fair when no individual's ball can be used on consecutive holes.

A variation is to make the JV players part of the competition for a half point.

WOLF ♟

**ONE PLAYER PICKS A TEAMMATE TO CHALLENGE
OTHERS ON ROTATING HOLES**

A single player goes against his opponents with a
partner or alone on designated holes. Before play
begins, decide on the tee off order and a dollar value for
points. Two points are at stake for each hole.

Players rotate the first player to tee off on each hole.
So in a foursome, a player tees off first every fourth
hole. The first player to tee off is the **Wolf**. The order
to tee off after the Wolf is dictated by honors according
to net scores on the previous hole. This insures that no
player has an advantage by the rotation. (Good idea to
circle your driving Wolf holes on the scorecard so you
don't get confused.) As the Wolf watches each of the
remaining players tee off, he may choose one person as
a playing partner. He must choose before the next
person hits. After all players have hit their drives, the
Wolf may choose to be a **Lone Wolf** if he is not
impressed with his opponent's drives.

The single best net score wins the points for the hole.
If the Wolf chooses a partner and one of them wins,
each player gets a point. A Lone Wolf who wins gets two
points for himself. Carry-overs are optional.

A variation is called PIG. In this game the person
teeing off first picks a partner after the 2nd shot on Par 4s
and 3 shot on Par 5s.

PART 3
Large Group Games

FUN FOR MULTIPLE FOURSOMES

AVERAGE SCORE

MULTIPLE TEAMS TRY TO WIN BY AVERAGING THEIR COMBINED SCORES ON EACH HOLE

Two- or four-person teams play against the rest of the competitors using their individual gross scores as a means of determining their team score. Each player's score is added to their partners and divided by the number on the team to establish an average that becomes the team score for the hole.

After completing the round, one-half of the team's combined handicap (1/4 of handicaps for four person teams) is deducted from their 18-hole total to determine their net score. Half strokes count as whole strokes after totaling. Competition is won or lost by comparing the difference in the team net scores. The game could designed around a Nassau format or even modified for Match Play.

BLIND PARTNERS

FIND OUT WHO YOUR TEAMMATE IS AFTER THE ROUND IS FINISHED

Play a competitive round and find out how you did when your partner is revealed at the end of the round. A blind draw from names in a hat at the conclusion of the round pairs people up. The group for the day agrees on a dollar buy-in for the pot. The number of teams is unlimited.

Several scoring variations are possible, limited only by your imagination. Common choices are: net best ball, net and gross best ball, aggregate, and match play. You can also add various points to win. (KP, Sandies, etc.)

Pay outs can be for the winners only, or with a large group pay for win, place and show.

THE BLIND "PROFIT"

TEAMMATES PREDICT THEIR SCORES AND PLAY IN SEPARATE GROUPS

This game is played with multiple foursomes where teammates must play in separate groups. The goal is to predict your team's combined score before the match begins.

Any scoring combination can be used: net, gross, best ball, combined score, etc. The winner will be the team to guess exactly right, or closest to their prediction either above or below.

Before play begins, teammates are selected and meet to decide what their score will be for the day. Their predicted score is then written on a piece of paper and stored in secret for comparison at the conclusion of match. Having partners in separate groups adds to the suspense and eliminates any chance of collaborative shot making on the final holes.

Another way to control the possibility of "cheating" is to say that anyone posting a double bogey or higher on the last two holes is disqualified.

CAPTURE THE FLAG

PLANT A FLAG ON THE COURSE WHEN YOU REACH THE NUMBER OF STROKES EQUAL TO PAR + YOUR HANDICAP

Players compete in **stroke play** where the object is to carry a flag around the course as far as possible. How far players get to carry their flag is determined by the number of strokes allocated to them. This is determined by adding par for the course to their handicap. For example, if the course rating is 72 and the handicap is 12, stroke allocation is 84. Once players have completed the number of strokes equal to par plus their handicap, they plant their flag. (If you're on the green, place the flag on the edge. In the rough, plant it on the edge of the fairway.)

If a competitor passes your flag with strokes remaining, he captures it. The last flag placed is the winner. (It's especially fun to plant your flag on the 19th hole!)

If more than one player still holds his flag at the conclusion of the round, the winner is the player who has the most remaining handicap strokes. For fun, you can also handle this situation by marking off one club length for each remaining stroke from a designated location off the 18th green (preferably in public view). A playoff method should be agreed to before the round starts in the event two players complete their rounds with the exact same remaining strokes.

COLOR BALL

**A SPECIALLY MARKED BALL IS PLAYED FOR ONE
SCORE ALONG WITH A TEAM BEST BALL**

To win this game a team must accumulate a best ball
score while protecting a colored ball that must be
played on a rotating basis by each player. Begin the
game by either bringing a colored ball, or clearly
marking a ball for each team.

Scoring on each hole is one best ball combined with
the score from the player hitting the color, or marked
ball. Each player in the foursome must take a turn
playing the color ball in an alternating 4-hole basis. On
the last two holes, the team can elect which player they
want to play the color ball.

Playing either gross or net scores for either ball (or
both) is acceptable. An alternative format is to play
more than one net best ball. This puts more pressure
on the team to perform and makes the scoring more
interesting.

If the color ball is lost, the team automatically forfeits.

ELIMIDATE

....

TEAMS MUST USE ONE PLAYER'S SCORE, BUT ONLY ONCE IN FOUR HOLE ROTATION

This game is unique in the way it puts increasing pressure on a player who is not playing his best. To get started, after all players have completed the first hole, one player's net score is selected for the team score. On the next hole, one of the remaining 3 players must be chosen to post his net score. On the 3rd hole, one of the two players who have not posted must be selected, and finally on the 4th hole, only one player is left to post a score for the team.

Then the rotation starts again and continues in the same method, starting over at the completion of each four hole segment. For the 17th and 18th holes, the team may select any players score, but not the same one twice.

THE RYDER CUP

TEAM PLAY ALTERNATING SCORING METHOD EVERY SIX HOLES

Two-player teams play three separate six-hole matches. On the first six holes, the team's net best ball counts; for the next six holes, one net and one gross score are added together. On the final six holes, the average aggregate score (both scores divided by two) of the twosome is used. Betting can be on an individual hole (match play) basis where teams play to win the most holes. Or, each six-hole format can equal a separate bet to be won or lost.

This game can be used for small groups as well, but best played with a number of teams.

PART 4

For the Wild and Crazy

IF YOUR ROUNDS GET TOO ROUTINE,
PULL OUT THESE GAMES
TO REALLY SHAKE THEM UP!

ANIMALS

TOY ANIMALS ARE AWARDED FOR ON-COURSE "BOOFS"

Add some fun to your playing partners unique errant shots and reward them with various animals representing the perils encountered. Some of the more popular choices are: **Monkeys** for hitting a tree; **Snakes** for three putting; **Camels** for landing in a sand trap; **Donkeys** for going out of bounds; and a **Fish** for going in the lake. Animals are passed to the unlucky player as soon as a shot qualifies during the round. The goal is to get off the 18th green with out possessing any animals. A dollar value is assigned to each animal. The player who owns the animal at the end of the round owes that amount to each of their opponents (or to the pot for multiple teams).

CADDY SHACK

WATCH YOUR OPPONENT MAKE A MISTAKE AND HE BECOMES YOUR CADDY.

This is a fun game for embarrassing your buddies. Everyone starts from the first tee on an equal basis, but once someone starts making mistakes, the fun begins.

- Beat your opponent on a hole and he gets to carry your bag on the next one.
- Watch your opponent three putt and he gets to fix every ball mark you can find on the green.
- Should he be unlucky enough to lose to you by two or more strokes, he not only gets to carry your bag, but he also gets to use a towel to clean all your clubs on the next tee.
- The winner of the entire 18 holes will have his clubs cleaned and bags carried to the car while he waits in the clubhouse for his caddy to buy the first drink.

The game can be played either gross or net and you can add some betting points (page 13) to make it even more interesting.

THE HAT

EMBARRASS YOUR BUDDIES AND GET FREE DRINKS

Bring the oldest, ugliest, gaudiest hat you can find to play this game. Any player in the foursome that three putts is required to wear the hat starting on the hole where the transgression occurred.

You are allowed to remove the hat only under two conditions: 1) by making a net birdie on a subsequent hole, or 2) by awarding it to a playing partner who next three putts. The unlucky person who is wearing the hat at the end of the round is required to wear it into the clubhouse until he buys all playing partners a drink. A three footer on number 18 never looked so long!

MAFIA

WIN HOLES AND STEAL YOUR OPPONENTS EQUIPMENT

A match play game where winning a hole means you score a point, but just as importantly, get to "steal" a club from your partner. (Putters are exempt.)

When a player's best net score wins a hole, he may choose to remove any club in his opponent's bag. The loser can reclaim clubs one at a time while simultaneously claiming one of the opponent's club as soon as he wins a hole. No clubs are exchanged on halved holes.

Knowing your opponents strengths and weaknesses can help create a careful strategy to pick the best club to "steal".

NEVADA

PARTNERS CREATE A HOLE SCORE BY COMBINING THE DIGITS OF THEIR INDIVIDUAL SCORE.

Get out your wallets on this one. Points can be won or lost in large numbers, so be careful with the value you place on each point. Using full handicaps, players record their best net scores as a two-digit number. (4 and a 5 = 45) Oh, there is one little exception: if neither teammate scores a net par or better, the team must place its higher score first. (For example: on a Par 4, a 5 and a 6 = 65.) 9 is the maximum allowed individual score on any one hole. (Just pick it up!) Scores are recorded after each hole and totaled for 18. The team with the fewest points wins and is paid off for the value of the point difference.

YARDAGE

THE NUMBER OF YARDS ON A HOLE WON IS YOUR SCORE

Like the game of Nevada, Yardage can become very expensive if you aren't careful with the dollar value placed on points. Best played with net scores, players or teams are awarded points equal the number of yards on each hole won. No points are awarded for halved holes and there are no carryovers.

For example, if you win a 550 yard Par 5, the points won are 550. If you are betting $1 per point, that's a cool $550. Ok, so maybe 10 cents might be a little safer? Make that Par 5 worth $55. Still swallowing hard? A penny a point makes loss of this hole a mere $5.50.

Some variations can make it more interesting, but more risky as well. You can agree at the start of the game that if an opponent falls behind by a certain number of points, he is allowed to 1) double the point value, and/or 2) call for carryovers.

A FINAL WORD

Golf is a wonderful game for life. It can also be a most frustrating experience. To me it's all about keeping it in perspective and managing expectations. The best book I ever read to learn these skills is Scott Peck's *Golf and The Spirit*.

Scott says, *"Learning to how to play golf with the slightest decency or pleasure has been a constant battle against my own personality. This has made me an expert. An expert on how not to play golf...."*

How many of us can relate to this statement!

Much can be learned about a person's character while playing a round of golf with them. How they see life and those around them often exposes itself during four hours on a golf course. One can easily observe another's competitiveness, patience, courteousness and ability to deal with pressure to name just a few. I've heard it said that one who cheats to keep a low handicap has an "insecurity complex", and one who cheats to maintain a higher handicap to win more bets has a "scarcity complex." Oh the psychology of it all....

Include a few of the games shared in this book and add another source of measurement to the mix!

ACKNOWLEDGMENTS

My interest in golf started when my dad took me along with a friend of his to play my first round of golf when I was twelve. I will never forget the feeling of satisfaction the first time I ever got the ball is the air. And then there were my buddies, Knabber, Dave, Rick, Ross, and Jake who challenged me to try to master the game. Being crazy enough to think I could write a book came from observing my former boss, Maury, who was the consummate dreamer.

I really appreciate all the people who shared their favorite golf games with me. My clients who encouraged me to take a risk. My daughter Cori helped along the way and inspired me to keep going. My son Kyle, who is my technical advisor, was always ready whenever I needed him. And my mom, Maxine helped me by typing first drafts.

Special thanks to the Willamette Valley Country Club gang who inspired me to write the book. The greatest group of guys you'd ever want to play with! Bob, Tim, Warren, Bill, Paul, Wayne, Charlie, Shawn, Shel, Larry, Ron, Fred, Todd, Dave, Russ, and Dan to name a few. Every Saturday we meet for breakfast and plan the day's match. The responsibility to organize a side game rotates by edict of Bob, "the commissioner". It's a lot of fun, and made me think what a great idea it would be to have a pocket reference of games and that maybe others would too.

....

And I couldn't have published the book without the generous support of my good friends at the design firm Bailey/Franklin (www.baileyfranklin.com), and Kelli Sussman of Consistent Image (www.consistentimage.com) who did the web site production.

Finally, thanks to Paulette Jarvey, Stephen Abouaf, Frank Petterson, and Ken Panck for being my entrepreneurial coaches!

So here it is. I hope you enjoy using this book to add more fun to your groups play!

To order additional copies of *Your Pocket Guide to Great Games for Golf*, visit www.greatgamesforgolf.com.

GLOSSARY

Visit www.greatgamesforgolf.com for a glossary of commonly used terms for golf games.